JELL-O® & Cool Whip® Whipped Topping

Simply *Delicious*

Publications International, Ltd.

Favorite Brand Name Recipes at www.fbnr.com

Desserts & Snacks Division Promotions Manager: Carol D. Harris
Kraft Kitchens Consumer Foods Manager: Normajean Longfield

Photography: Stephen Hamilton Photographics, Inc.
Photographers: Stephen Hamilton, Tate Hunt
Prop Stylist: Paula Walters
Food Stylists: Tobe LeMoine, Walter Moeller
Assistant Food Stylist: Susie Skoog

Pictured on the front cover *(left to right):* Citrus Parfaits *(page 76)* and Strawberry Margarita Pie *(page 67)*.

Pictured on the back cover: Lemon-Blueberry Pie Cups *(page 54)*.

ISBN: 0-7853-5429-8

Manufactured in China.

8 7 6 5 4 3 2 1

Nutritional Analysis: Nutritional information is given for some of the recipes in this publication. Each analysis is based on the food items in the ingredient list, except ingredients labeled as "optional" or "for garnish." When more than one ingredient choice is listed, the first ingredient is used for analysis. If a range for the amount of an ingredient is given, the nutritional analysis is based on the lowest amount. Foods offered as "serve with" suggestions are not included in the analysis unless otherwise stated.

Preparation/Cooking Times: Preparation times are based on the approximate amount of time required to assemble the recipe before cooking, baking, chilling or serving. These times include preparation steps such as measuring, chopping and mixing. The fact that some preparations and cooking can be done simultaneously is taken into account. Preparation of optional ingredients and serving suggestions is not included.

Contents

www.jell-o.com   www.coolwhip.com

I could go for something JELL-O® Tips & Techniques

All of the recipes appearing in this publication have been developed and tested by the food professionals in the Kraft Kitchens to ensure your success in making them. We also share our JELL-O secrets with you. These foolproof tips, many with step-by-step photos, help you get perfect results every time.

Gelatin

Making JELL-O Brand Gelatin Dessert is easy. Just follow the package directions and the results will be a success.

The basic directions as written below are also on the package:

• Stir 1 cup boiling water into 1 package (4-serving size) gelatin at least 2 minutes until completely dissolved. Stir in 1 cup cold water. Refrigerate 4 hours or until firm. (For an 8-serving size package, use 2 cups boiling water and 2 cups cold water.)

• JELL-O Brand Sugar Free Low Calorie Gelatin Dessert is prepared in the same way. It can be used in many recipes that call for JELL-O Brand Gelatin Dessert.

Some tips for success
• To make a mixture that is clear and uniformly set, be sure the gelatin is completely dissolved in boiling water or other boiling liquid before adding the cold water.

• To double a recipe, just double the amounts of gelatin, liquid and other ingredients used, except salt, vinegar and lemon juice. For these, use 1½ times the amount given in the recipe.

• To store prepared gelatin overnight or longer, cover it before refrigerating to prevent drying. Always store gelatin desserts and molds in the refrigerator.

• Generally, gelatin molds are best served right from the refrigerator. A gelatin mold containing fruit or vegetables can remain at room temperature up to 2 hours. Always keep a gelatin mold containing meat, mayonnaise, ice cream or other dairy products refrigerated until ready to serve. Store any leftover gelatin mold in the refrigerator.

Gelatin Refrigerating Time Chart

In all recipes, for best results, the gelatin needs to be refrigerated to the proper consistency. Use this chart as a guideline to determine the desired consistency and the approximate refrigerating time.

When a recipe says:	It means gelatin should:	Refrigerating Time:		Gelatin Uses:
		Regular set	Speed set*	
"Refrigerate until syrupy"	Be consistency of thick syrup	1 hour	3 minutes	Glaze for pies, fruit
"Refrigerate until slightly thickened"	Be consistency of unbeaten egg whites	1¼ hours	5 to 6 minutes	Adding creamy ingredients or when mixture will be beaten
"Refrigerate until thickened"	Be thick enough so that a spoon drawn through leaves a definite impression	1½ hours	7 to 8 minutes	Adding solid ingredients such as fruits or vegetables
"Refrigerate until set but not firm"	Stick to finger when touched and should mound or move to the side when bowl or mold is tilted	2 hours	30 minutes	Layering gelatin mixtures
"Refrigerate until firm"	Not stick to finger when touched and not mound or move when mold is tilted	Individual molds: at least 3 hours 2- to 6-cup mold: at least 4 hours 8- to 12-cup mold: at least 5 hours or overnight		Unmolding and serving

Speed set (ice cube) method is not recommended for molding.

The Secret to Molding Gelatin

The Mold
• Use metal molds, traditional decorative molds and other metal forms, or plastic molds. You can use square or round cake pans, fluted or plain tube pans, loaf pans, or metal mixing bowls (the nested sets give you a variety of sizes). You can also use metal fruit or juice cans. (To unmold, dip can in warm water, then puncture bottom of can and unmold.)

• To determine the volume of the mold, measure first with water. Most recipes give an indication of the size of the mold needed. For clear gelatin, you need a 2-cup mold for a 4-serving size package and a 4-cup mold for an 8-serving size package.

• If a mold holds less than the size called for, pour the extra gelatin into a separate dish. Refrigerate and serve it at another time. Do not use a mold that is too large, since it would be difficult to unmold. Either increase the recipe or use a smaller mold.

• For easier unmolding, spray mold with no stick cooking spray before filling mold.

The Preparation
• To prepare gelatin for molding, use less water than the amount called for on the package. For a 4-serving size package, decrease cold water to ¾ cup. For an 8-serving size package, decrease cold water to 1½ cups. (This adjustment has already been made in the recipes in this publication.) The firmer consistency will result in a less fragile mold. It also makes unmolding much simpler.

• To arrange fruits or vegetables in the mold, refrigerate gelatin until thickened. (If gelatin is not thick enough, fruits or vegetables may sink or float.) Pour gelatin into mold to about ¼-inch depth. Reserve remaining gelatin at room temperature. Arrange fruits or vegetables in decorative pattern on gelatin. Refrigerate mold until gelatin is set but not firm. Spoon reserved gelatin over pattern in mold. Refrigerate until firm, then unmold.

The Unmolding
• First, allow gelatin to set until firm by refrigerating several hours or overnight. Also chill serving plate on which mold is to be served by storing in refrigerator.

• Make certain that gelatin is completely firm. It should not feel sticky on top and should not mound or move to the side if mold is tilted.

• Moisten tips of fingers and gently pull gelatin from around edge of mold. Or, use a small metal spatula or pointed knife dipped in warm water to loosen top edge.

• Dip mold in warm, not hot, water just to rim for about 15 seconds. Lift

from water, hold upright and shake to loosen gelatin. Or, gently pull gelatin from edge of mold.

• Moisten chilled serving plate with water. (This allows gelatin to be moved after unmolding.) Place moistened serving plate on top of mold. Invert mold and plate; holding mold and plate together, shake slightly to loosen. Gently remove mold. If gelatin does not release easily, dip mold in warm water again for a few seconds. Center gelatin on serving plate.

How to Unmold Gelatin

1. Before unmolding, gently pull gelatin from around edge of mold with moist fingertips.

2. Dip mold in warm water, just to the rim, for about 15 seconds.

3. Lift mold from water, hold upright and shake to loosen gelatin.

4. Place moistened serving plate on top of mold.

5. Invert mold and plate; shake to loosen gelatin.

6. Remove mold and center gelatin on plate.

Pudding

The recipes in this publication use both JELL-O Cook & Serve Pudding & Pie Filling, which requires cooking, and JELL-O Instant Pudding & Pie Filling, which is not cooked. These products are not interchangeable in recipes. Be sure to use the product called for in the recipe.

JELL-O Instant Pudding & Pie Filling is also available Fat Free. Both the Instant and the Cook & Serve Pudding & Pie Fillings are also available as Sugar Free Fat Free.

See individual packages for basic directions for preparing the products as either a pudding or a pie filling.

Some Tips for Success
For JELL-O Instant Pudding & Pie Filling:

• Always use cold milk. Beat pudding mix slowly, not vigorously.

• For best results, use 2% reduced fat milk or whole milk. Fat free, 1% lowfat, reconstituted nonfat dry milk or lactose-reduced milk can also be used. For Fat Free or Sugar Free Fat Free Pudding & Pie Filling, use cold fat free milk.

• Always store prepared pudding desserts, pies and snacks in the refrigerator.

For JELL-O Cook & Serve Pudding & Pie Filling:

• It's best to cook the pudding in a heavy saucepan to ensure even heating. Stir pudding mixture constantly as it cooks. Make sure it comes to a full boil. The mixture will be thin, but will thicken as it cools.

• For a creamier pudding, place a piece of plastic wrap on the surface of pudding while cooling. Stir before serving.

• To cool pudding quickly, place saucepan of hot pudding in larger pan of ice water; stir frequently until mixture is cooled. Do not use this method for pie filling.

No Bake Cheesecakes & Desserts
Some Tips for Success

• The cheesecake can also be prepared in an 8- or 9-inch square pan or 12 foil- or paper-lined muffin cups.

• Two packages of the cheesecake can be prepared in a 13×9-inch pan or a 9×3-inch springform pan.

• To serve, dip the pie plate just to the rim in hot water for 30 seconds before cutting.

• To freeze, cover the cheesecake. Freeze up to 2 weeks. Thaw in refrigerator 3 hours before serving.

• For easy cleanup, line the 8- or 9-inch square pan with foil before preparing the No Bake Dessert.

• The No Bake Desserts can also be served frozen. Freeze 4 hours or until firm. Remove from freezer and serve immediately.

Do The Cool Whip!™
Cool Whip Whipped Topping Tips & Techniques

Make every day a day to remember. With COOL WHIP Whipped Topping, whether you are looking for a tasty tidbit or a divine dessert, the perfect recipe for all your celebrations is just around the corner. From classic holiday recipes to everyday snacking ideas, you'll discover that COOL WHIP is more than just a topping.

How Much COOL WHIP to Use

COOL WHIP Whipped Topping comes in 3 sizes. To estimate recipe needs, the number of cups per tub is listed in the chart below.

Tub size	Cool Whip Regular Amount	Cool Whip Extra Creamy Amount	Cool Whip Lite/Free Amount
8 ounces	3 cups	3 cups	3$\frac{1}{4}$ cups
12 ounces	4$\frac{1}{2}$ cups	4$\frac{1}{2}$ cups	5 cups
16 ounces	6$\frac{3}{4}$ cups	– – –	6$\frac{1}{2}$ cups*

* COOL WHIP Free is not available in a 16 ounce tub.

Working with COOL WHIP

How To Thaw COOL WHIP
Place tub of COOL WHIP Whipped Topping, unopened, in the refrigerator. For complete thawing, allow these times:

- 4 hours for 8-ounce tub
- 5 hours for 12-ounce tub
- 6 hours for 16-ounce tub

Do not thaw COOL WHIP in the microwave.

How to Store COOL WHIP
- For long-term storage, keep COOL WHIP Whipped Topping in the freezer.

- Once thawed, refrigerate for no more than 2 weeks, or re-freeze.

- Don't let the container stand in a hot kitchen—the topping will soften and begin to liquify.

- Desserts prepared with COOL WHIP Whipped Topping should be stored in the refrigerator or freezer.

How to Use COOL WHIP
- COOL WHIP Regular, Extra Creamy and COOL WHIP Lite Whipped Toppings can usually be used interchangeably in recipes. When used with gelatin or high-acid fruits, COOL WHIP Lite may produce a softer set.

- COOL WHIP Free is not interchangeable with all the recipes in this magazine. When substituting COOL WHIP Free, the end result will be a very soft set and slightly lower volume.

- Drain thawed frozen fruit before serving with COOL WHIP. The juice may make the topping appear curdled.

- COOL WHIP Whipped Topping can be substituted for an equal amount of whipped cream. If the recipe calls for liquid cream to be whipped, simply double the amount of liquid cream called for and substitute that amount of COOL WHIP.

- Thaw COOL WHIP Whipped Topping completely before measuring or stirring into ingredients.

- COOL WHIP Whipped Topping can be scooped like ice cream directly from the tub while still frozen.

- Completely thawed COOL WHIP Whipped Topping can be spooned into a pastry bag or decorating tube and piped decoratively like whipped cream or frosting.

Easy Garnishes with COOL WHIP

Whipped Topping Dollops

1. *Swirl spoon, held upright, through thawed COOL WHIP, creating rippled surface on the whipped topping.*

2. *Dip spoon into rippled whipped topping to scoop up heaping spoonful of whipped topping, maintaining rippled surface.*

3. *Gently touch spoon onto surface of dessert and release whipped topping gradually onto surface, pulling spoon up into a crowning tip.*

Whipped Topping Piping

Insert decorating tip into pastry bag; fill with thawed COOL WHIP Whipped Topping.

Fold down pastry bag. Holding bag firmly with one hand and squeezing topping down into tip, guide tip around surface to be decorated. If desired, double back whipped topping at intervals for decorative wave effect.

I could go for something

JELL-O ®
BRAND

Do The Cool Whip! ™

Whipped Topping

The Lighter Side

Café Ladyfinger Dessert

2 packages (3 ounces each) ladyfingers, split, separated
1 cup freshly brewed strong MAXWELL HOUSE *or* YUBAN Coffee,
**   any variety, at room temperature, divided**
1 package (8 ounces) PHILADELPHIA FREE Fat Free Cream Cheese
2 cups cold fat free milk
2 packages (4-serving size each) JELL-O Vanilla Flavor Fat Free
**   Sugar Free Instant Reduced Calorie Pudding & Pie Filling**
1 tub (8 ounces) COOL WHIP FREE Whipped Topping, thawed,
**   divided**

BRUSH cut side of ladyfingers with about ¼ cup of the coffee. Place ladyfingers on bottom and up side of 2-quart serving bowl.

BEAT cream cheese and remaining ¾ cup coffee in large bowl with wire whisk until smooth. Gradually beat in milk until smooth. Add pudding mixes. Beat with wire whisk 1 minute or until well blended. Gently stir in ½ of the whipped topping. Spoon into prepared bowl; cover.

continued on page 16

Café Ladyfinger Dessert, *continued*

REFRIGERATE 1 hour or until ready to serve. Top with remaining whipped topping. *Makes 12 servings*

Special Extra: *Garnish with 3 tablespoons shaved or chopped chocolate. (Nutrition will vary.)*

Prep: 20 minutes   **Refrigerate:** 1 hour

Nutrition Information Per Serving: *110 calories, 1.5g saturated fat, 30mg cholesterol, 360mg sodium, 19g carbohydrate, 0g dietary fiber, 5g protein*

Exchange: *1½ Starch*

Yogurt Crunch Parfaits

1 container (8 ounces) BREYERS Lowfat Yogurt, any flavor
1 tub (8 ounces) COOL WHIP FREE *or* COOL WHIP LITE Whipped
   Topping, thawed, divided
1 banana, sliced
1 can (20 ounces) pineapple chunks, drained
1 cup POST SELECTS Banana Nut Crunch Cereal

STIR yogurt and ½ of the whipped topping in large bowl until smooth. Alternately layer yogurt mixture, banana, pineapple chunks, cereal and remaining whipped topping in 6 parfait glasses; repeat layers.
Makes 6 servings

Great Substitute: *Use your favorite fruit and POST cereal as a substitute. (Nutrition will vary.)*

Prep: 5 minutes

Nutrition Information Per Serving: *220 calories, 2.5g saturated fat, <5mg cholesterol, 80mg sodium, 48g carbohydrate, 2g dietary fiber, 3g protein*

Exchange: *3 Carbohydrate*

Cookies and Creme Snacks

2 cups reduced fat chocolate wafer cookie crumbs
1 tub (12 ounces) COOL WHIP FREE Whipped Topping, thawed

STIR cookie crumbs into whipped topping. Spoon into snack cups.

REFRIGERATE or freeze until ready to serve.

Makes 13 ($\frac{1}{2}$-cup) servings

Great Substitute: *Prepare as directed above, substituting 2 cups raspberries or chopped strawberries for cookies. (Nutrition will vary.)*

Prep: 5 minutes

Nutrition Information Per Serving: *130 calories, 1.5g saturated fat, 0mg cholesterol, 100mg sodium, 26g carbohydrate, 0g dietary fiber, 2g protein*

Exchange: *$\frac{1}{2}$ Fat*

Juicy JELL-O®

1 cup boiling water
1 package (4-serving size) JELL-O Brand Strawberry Flavor Sugar Free Low Calorie Gelatin
1 cup cold orange juice

STIR boiling water into gelatin in medium bowl at least 2 minutes until completely dissolved. Stir in orange juice.

REFRIGERATE 4 hours or until firm.   *Makes 4 ($\frac{1}{2}$-cup) servings*

Prep: 5 minutes   **Refrigerate:** 4 hours

Nutrition Information Per Serving: *35 calories, 0g saturated fat, 0mg cholesterol, 60mg sodium, 6g carbohydrate, 0g dietary fiber, 2g protein*

Exchange: *$\frac{1}{2}$ Fruit*

Chocolate Banana Parfaits

2 cups cold fat free milk
1 package (4-serving size) JELL-O Chocolate Flavor Fat Free Sugar
Free Instant Reduced Calorie Pudding & Pie Filling
2 medium bananas, sliced
½ cup thawed COOL WHIP LITE Whipped Topping
1 tablespoon chopped walnuts

POUR milk into medium bowl. Add pudding mix. Beat with wire whisk 1 minute.

SPOON ½ of the pudding evenly into 4 dessert glasses. Layer with banana slices, whipped topping and remaining pudding.

REFRIGERATE until ready to serve. Garnish each serving with additional banana slices, whipped topping and walnuts, if desired.

Makes 4 servings

Great Substitute: *For a really great twist, prepare as directed above, substituting JELL-O Vanilla Flavor Fat Free Sugar Free Instant Reduced Calorie Pudding & Pie Filling for the Chocolate Flavor and drizzle each serving with 1 teaspoon KRAFT Caramel Topping. (Nutrition will vary.)*

Prep: 5 minutes

Nutrition Information Per Serving: *(without additional garnish)* 160 calories, 1.5g saturated fat, <5mg cholesterol, 380mg sodium, 30g carbohydrate, 2g dietary fiber, 6g protein

Exchange: ½ Fat

Chocolate Banana Parfait

Florida Sunshine Cups

¾ **cup boiling water**
1 **package (4-serving size) JELL-O Brand Orange *or* Lemon Flavor Sugar Free Low Calorie Gelatin**
1 **cup cold orange juice**
½ **cup fresh raspberries**
1 **can (11 ounces) mandarin orange segments, drained**

STIR boiling water into gelatin in large bowl at least 2 minutes until completely dissolved. Stir in cold juice. Refrigerate 1½ hours or until thickened (spoon drawn through leaves definite impression).

MEASURE ¾ cup thickened gelatin into medium bowl; set aside. Stir fruit into remaining gelatin. Pour into serving bowl or 6 dessert dishes.

BEAT reserved gelatin with electric mixer on high speed until fluffy and about doubled in volume. Spoon over gelatin in bowl or dishes.

REFRIGERATE 3 hours or until firm. *Makes 6 servings*

Prep: 20 minutes   **Refrigerate:** 4½ hours

Nutrition Information Per Serving: *20 calories, 0g saturated fat, 0mg cholesterol, 45mg sodium, 3g carbohydrate, <1g dietary fiber, 1g protein*

Exchange: *Free*

Florida Sunshine Cups

Mocha Pudding Parfaits

1½ **cups cold fat free milk**
1 **tablespoon MAXWELL HOUSE Instant Coffee**
1 **package (4-serving size) JELL-O Chocolate Flavor Fat Free Sugar Free Instant Reduced Calorie Pudding & Pie Filling**
1 **tub (8 ounces) COOL WHIP FREE Whipped Topping, thawed, divided**
6 **reduced fat chocolate wafer cookies, chopped**

POUR milk and coffee into medium bowl. Add pudding mix. Beat with wire whisk 1 minute. Gently stir in ½ of the whipped topping.

SPOON ½ of the pudding mixture evenly into 6 dessert dishes. Sprinkle with chopped cookies. Top with ½ of the remaining whipped topping. Top with remaining pudding mixture. Garnish each serving with a spoonful of remaining whipped topping.

REFRIGERATE until ready to serve.   *Makes 6 servings*

Great Substitute: *The coffee can be omitted. Drizzle each serving with 1 teaspoon fat free chocolate syrup for a really indulgent treat! (Nutrition will vary.)*

Prep: 10 minutes

Nutrition Information Per Serving: *130 calories, 2g saturated fat, 0mg cholesterol, 280mg sodium, 26g carbohydrate, 1g dietary fiber, 3g protein*

Exchange: *½ Fat*

Mocha Pudding Parfaits

I could go for something

Mold Mania

Apple Blossom Mold

1½ cups boiling water
1 package (8-serving size) *or* 2 packages (4-serving size each)
    JELL-O Brand Lemon Flavor Gelatin
2 cups cold apple juice
1 cup diced red and green apples

STIR boiling water into gelatin in large bowl at least 2 minutes until completely dissolved. Stir in cold juice. Refrigerate about 1½ hours or until thickened (spoon drawn through leaves definite impression). Stir in apples. Pour into 6-cup mold which has been sprayed with no stick cooking spray.

REFRIGERATE 4 hours or until firm. Unmold. Garnish as desired.

Makes 10 servings

Variation: *Sugar Free Low Calorie Gelatin may be substituted.*

Prep: 15 minutes   **Refrigerate:** 5½ hours

Juicy Layered Orange Pineapple Mold

1 can (20 ounces) crushed pineapple in juice, undrained
Cold orange juice
1½ cups boiling water
1 package (8-serving size) *or* 2 packages (4-serving size each)
    JELL-O Brand Orange Flavor Gelatin
1 package (8 ounces) PHILADELPHIA Cream Cheese, softened

DRAIN pineapple, reserving juice. Add cold orange juice to pineapple juice to make 1½ cups. Stir boiling water into gelatin in large bowl at least 2 minutes until completely dissolved. Stir in measured juice. Reserve 1 cup gelatin at room temperature.

STIR ½ of the crushed pineapple into remaining gelatin. Pour into 6-cup mold which has been sprayed with no stick cooking spray. Refrigerate about 2 hours or until set but not firm (should stick to finger when touched and should mound).

STIR reserved gelatin gradually into cream cheese in medium bowl with wire whisk until smooth. Stir in remaining crushed pineapple. Spoon over gelatin layer in mold.

REFRIGERATE 4 hours or until firm. Unmold. Garnish as desired.
Makes 10 servings

Take a Shortcut: *Soften cream cheese in microwave on HIGH 15 to 20 seconds.*

Prep: 20 minutes   **Refrigerate:** 6 hours

Juicy Layered Orange Pineapple Mold

Under the Sea Mold

**1 can (15.25 ounces) pineapple sea creatures fun shapes,
   undrained**
1½ cups boiling water, divided
1 package (4-serving size) JELL-O Brand Lime Flavor Gelatin
1 package (4-serving size) JELL-O Brand Lemon Flavor Gelatin
1 cup cold water
Ice cubes

DRAIN pineapple; reserve ½ cup juice.

STIR ¾ cup of boiling water into each flavor of gelatin in separate medium bowls at least 2 minutes until completely dissolved. Stir cold water into lime gelatin. Refrigerate 45 minutes or until slightly thickened (consistency of unbeaten egg whites).

MEANWHILE, mix pineapple juice and ice cubes to make 1 cup. Add to lemon flavor gelatin, stirring until slightly thickened. Stir in ½ of the pineapple shapes. Pour into 5-cup mold which has been sprayed with no stick cooking spray. Refrigerate 40 minutes or until set but not firm (should stick to finger when touched).

STIR remaining pineapple shapes into thickened lime gelatin. Spoon over lemon gelatin in mold.

REFRIGERATE 4 hours or until firm. Unmold.

Makes 10 servings

Prep: 15 minutes   **Refrigerate:** 5½ hours

Sparkling Tropical Fruit Mold

1½ cups boiling white grape juice
1 package (6 ounces) *or* 2 packages (3 ounces each) JELL-O Brand
    Sparkling White Grape Flavor Gelatin
2 cups cold club soda or seltzer
1 can (15.25 ounces) tropical fruit salad, drained, chopped
½ cup dried cranberries

STIR boiling juice into gelatin in large bowl at least 2 minutes until completely dissolved. Refrigerate 15 minutes. Gently stir in cold club soda. Refrigerate 30 minutes or until slightly thickened (consistency of unbeaten egg whites). Gently stir tropical fruit salad and cranberries into gelatin. Spoon into 6-cup mold which has been sprayed with no stick cooking spray; cover.

REFRIGERATE 4 hours or until firm. Unmold. Garnish as desired.

Makes 12 servings

Prep: 15 minutes   **Refrigerate:** 4¾ hours

Great Substitute

*Golden raisins may be substituted for
the dried cranberries.*

Peaches and Cream Mold

1½ **cups boiling water**
  1 **package (8-serving size)** *or* **2 packages (4-serving size each)**
    JELL-O Brand Peach *or* **Orange Flavor Gelatin**
1½ **cups cold water**
  1 **tub (8 ounces) COOL WHIP Whipped Topping, thawed, divided**
  1 **can (16 ounces) peach slices in syrup, drained, diced**

STIR boiling water into gelatin in large bowl at least 2 minutes until completely dissolved. Stir in cold water. Refrigerate about 1¼ hours or until slightly thickened (consistency of unbeaten egg whites).

STIR in 2 cups whipped topping with wire whisk until smooth. Refrigerate about 15 minutes or until thickened (spoon drawn through leaves definite impression). Stir in peaches. Pour into 5-cup mold which has been sprayed with no stick cooking spray.

REFRIGERATE 4 hours or until firm. Unmold. Garnish as desired. Serve with remaining whipped topping.   *Makes 10 servings*

Prep: 15 minutes   **Refrigerate:** 5½ hours

Great Substitute

*1 cup fresh or thawed frozen
raspberries may be used in place
of the peaches.*

Peaches and Cream Mold

Juiced Up Fruit Mold

2½ **cups boiling water**
  1 **package (8-serving size)** *or* **2 packages (4-serving size each)**
    JELL-O Brand Gelatin, any red flavor
  1 **cup cold cranberry juice cocktail**
  1 **can (11 ounces) mandarin orange segments, drained**
  1 **cup halved seedless green grapes**

STIR boiling water into gelatin in large bowl at least 2 minutes until completely dissolved. Stir in cold juice. Refrigerate about 1½ hours or until thickened (spoon drawn through leaves definite impression). Stir in fruit. Spoon into 6-cup mold which has been sprayed with no stick cooking spray.

REFRIGERATE about 4 hours or until firm. Unmold.

Makes 10 servings

Prep: 20 minutes   **Refrigerate:** 5½ hours

Great Substitute

Other juices may be substituted for cranberry, except fresh or frozen pineapple, kiwi, papaya or guava juice. Gelatin will not set.

Juiced Up Fruit Mold

I could go for something

JELL-O® BRAND

Do The Cool Whip!™
Cool Whip® Whipped Topping

Spring Sensations

Cool Yogurt Smoothie

1 container (8 ounces) BREYERS Strawberry Lowfat Yogurt, any variety
½ tub (8 ounces) COOL WHIP Whipped Topping, thawed *or* frozen
1 cup fresh *or* frozen strawberries *or* any other seasonal fruit, chopped (optional)

PLACE yogurt, whipped topping and fruit in blender container; cover. Blend until smooth. (For thinner consistency, add ice cubes.) Serve immediately.

Makes 2 servings

Storage Know-How: *Smoothie can be covered and stored in the refrigerator up to 24 hours, or frozen up to 1 week. Reblend before serving. (Thaw frozen smoothie 20 minutes before blending.)*

Prep: 1 minute

Chocolate Passion Layered Dessert

4 cups cold milk
2 packages (4-serving size each) JELL-O Chocolate Flavor Instant Pudding & Pie Filling
1 package (12 ounces) pound cake, cut into cubes
¼ cup chocolate syrup or coffee liqueur, divided
1 package (12 ounces) BAKER'S Semi-Sweet Chocolate Chunks
1 tub (8 ounces) COOL WHIP Extra Creamy Whipped Topping, thawed

POUR milk into large bowl. Add pudding mixes. Beat with wire whisk 1 minute or until well blended.

PLACE ½ of the cake cubes in large glass serving bowl. Drizzle with ½ of the chocolate syrup. Spread ½ of the pudding over cake in bowl. Sprinkle ½ of the chunks over pudding. Spread with ½ of the whipped topping. Repeat layers. Refrigerate until ready to serve.

Makes 12 servings

Prep: 15 minutes

Great Substitute

For a really decadent dessert, use one baked brownie layer in place of the pound cake

Chocolate Passion Layered Dessert

White Chocolate-Raspberry Cheesecake

1½ **packages (3 ounces each) soft ladyfingers**
1 **package (8 ounces) PHILADELPHIA Cream Cheese, softened**
2 **cups cold milk, divided**
2 **packages (4-serving size each) JELL-O White Chocolate Flavor Instant Pudding & Pie Filling**
1 **tub (8 ounces) COOL WHIP Whipped Topping, thawed, divided**
¼ **cup seedless raspberry jam**

ARRANGE ladyfingers on side and bottom of 9-inch springform pan. In large bowl, beat cream cheese and ½ cup of the milk with electric mixer until smooth. Add remaining 1½ cups milk and pudding mixes. Beat until smooth. Stir in 1 cup of the whipped topping until smooth and well blended. Spoon into crust.

STIR remaining whipped topping and raspberry jam until just blended. Spread evenly over white chocolate layer. Garnish with additional whipped topping and fresh raspberries, if desired.

Makes 10 to 12 servings

Refrigerate: 4 hours

Great Substitute: *Instead of ladyfingers, line pan with thin slices of prepared pound cake, overlapping slightly.*

Variation: *For a citrusy twist, substitute lemon flavor instant pudding for the white chocolate flavor.*

Prep: 10 minutes   **Refrigerate:** 4 hours

Lemon Bars

    15 whole graham crackers
    2 packages (8 ounces each) PHILADELPHIA Cream Cheese,
       softened
    3½ cups cold milk
    3 packages (4-serving size each) JELL-O Lemon Flavor Instant
       Pudding & Pie Filling
    1 tub (8 ounces) COOL WHIP Whipped Topping, thawed, divided

ARRANGE ½ of the crackers in bottom of 13×9-inch pan, cutting crackers to fit, if necessary.

BEAT cream cheese in large bowl with electric mixer on low speed until smooth. Gradually beat in 1 cup of the milk. Add remaining milk and pudding mixes. Beat 1 to 2 minutes. (Mixture will be thick.) Gently stir in 2 cups of the whipped topping.

SPREAD ½ of the pudding mixture over crackers in pan. Arrange remaining crackers over pudding in pan. Top with remaining pudding mixture. Cover with remaining whipped topping. Refrigerate 4 hours or freeze 3 hours. Cut into bars. *Makes 18 servings*

Prep: 10 minutes   **Refrigerate:** 4 hours   **Freeze:** 3 hours

Best of the Season

*Garnish with fresh seasonal berries,
if desired.*

White Chocolate-Hazelnut Pie

2 cups cold milk
2 packages (4-serving size each) JELL-O White Chocolate Flavor
***or* other Chocolate Flavor Instant Pudding & Pie Filling**
1 envelope (.64 ounce) GENERAL FOODS INTERNATIONAL
COFFEES Hazelnut Flavor (about 2 tablespoons)
1 tub (8 ounces) COOL WHIP Whipped Topping, thawed, divided
1 prepared chocolate flavor *or* graham cracker crumb crust
(6 ounces or 9 inches)

POUR milk into medium bowl. Add pudding mixes and flavored instant coffee. Beat with wire whisk 1 minute or until well blended. (Mixture will be thick.) Gently stir in ½ of the whipped topping. Spoon evenly into crust. Spread remaining whipped topping over pudding in crust.

REFRIGERATE 3 hours or until set. Garnish as desired.

Makes 8 servings

Prep: 15 minutes   **Refrigerate:** 3 hours

Great Substitute

Substitute 2 to 3 teaspoons MAXWELL HOUSE Instant Coffee for GENERAL FOODS INTERNATIONAL COFFEES, Hazelnut Flavor.

White Chocolate-Hazelnut Pie

Dulce de Leche Frozen Dessert

3 cups half-and-half or milk
6 tablespoons KRAFT Caramel Topping, divided
1 package (4-serving size) JELL-O Butterscotch Flavor Instant
**   Pudding & Pie Filling**
1 package (4-serving size) JELL-O Vanilla Flavor Instant Pudding
**   & Pie Filling**
1 tub (8 ounces) COOL WHIP Whipped Topping, thawed

POUR half-and-half into large bowl. Stir in 2 tablespoons caramel topping until dissolved. Add pudding mixes. Beat with wire whisk 1 minute or until well blended. Gently stir in whipped topping until well mixed.

SPOON ½ of the pudding mixture into 8×4-inch loaf pan which has been lined with plastic wrap. Drizzle remaining caramel topping over mixture. Carefully spoon remaining pudding mixture over caramel and smooth with spatula.

FREEZE about 6 hours or overnight or until firm. Carefully invert pan onto serving platter and remove plastic wrap. Let stand at room temperature about 15 minutes before slicing.   *Makes 8 servings*

Variation: *To prepare individual Dulce de Leche frozen pops or cups, spoon ½ of the pudding mixture into 10 to 12 paper-lined muffin cups. Place teaspoonful of caramel topping in center of each cup and cover with remaining pudding mixture. For pops, stick wooden popsicle sticks into each cup and freeze.*

Prep: 20 minutes   **Freeze:** 6 hours

Fudge Bottom Cheesecake

1 package (11.1 ounces) JELL-O No Bake Real Cheesecake
2 tablespoons sugar
6 tablespoons butter or margarine, melted
1 tablespoon water
3 squares BAKER'S Semi-Sweet Baking Chocolate
1 tablespoon butter or margarine
1½ cups cold milk

STIR Crust Mix, sugar, melted butter and water thoroughly with fork in 9-inch pie plate until crumbs are well moistened. First press firmly against side of pie plate, using finger or measuring cup to shape edge. Press remaining crumbs firmly onto bottom, using measuring cup.

MICROWAVE chocolate and 1 tablespoon butter in small microwavable bowl on HIGH 1½ minutes or until chocolate is almost melted. Stir until completely melted; cool slightly.

BEAT milk and Filling Mix with electric mixer on lowest speed until blended. Beat on medium speed 3 minutes. (Filling will be thick.) Stir 3 tablespoons of the filling into melted chocolate until well blended. Spread evenly into crust. Top with remaining filling.

REFRIGERATE at least 1 hour. Garnish as desired.

Makes 8 servings

Fudge Bottom Cheesecake Tarts: *Using a spoon or bottom of glass, press prepared crust mixture firmly onto bottom of 12 paper-lined muffin cups. Prepare filling mixtures as directed above. Spread 1 heaping teaspoon of the chocolate mixture into each crust. Top with remaining filling. Refrigerate as directed.*   *Makes 12 servings*

Tip: *For ease in serving, dip bottom of pie plate in hot water for 10 to 15 seconds prior to slicing.*

Prep: 15 minutes   **Refrigerate:** 1 hour

Chocolate Toffee Bar Dessert

1 cup flour
½ cup pecans, toasted and finely chopped
¼ cup sugar
½ cup (1 stick) butter or margarine, melted
1 cup toffee bits, divided
2 cups cold milk
2 packages (4-serving size each) JELL-O Chocolate Flavor Instant
    Pudding & Pie Filling
1 tub (8 ounces) COOL WHIP Whipped Topping, thawed, divided

HEAT oven to 400°F.

MIX flour, pecans, sugar, butter and ½ cup of the toffee bits in large bowl until well mixed. Press firmly onto bottom of 13×9-inch pan. Bake 10 minutes or until lightly browned. Cool.

POUR milk into large bowl. Add pudding mixes. Beat with wire whisk 1 minute or until well blended. Spread 1½ cups pudding on bottom of crust.

GENTLY stir ½ of the whipped topping into remaining pudding. Spread over pudding in pan. Top with remaining whipped topping. Sprinkle with remaining toffee bits.

REFRIGERATE 3 hours or overnight.   *Makes 15 servings*

Great Substitute: *JELL-O Butterscotch Flavor Instant Pudding can be substituted for Chocolate Flavor with delicious results.*

Prep: 20 minutes   **Bake:** 10 minutes   **Refrigerate:** 3 hours

Chocolate Toffee Bar Dessert

Luscious Spring Poke Cake

2 baked 8- or 9-inch round white cake layers, cooled completely
2 cups boiling water
1 package (8-serving size) *or* 2 packages (4-serving size each) JELL-O Brand Gelatin, any flavor
1 tub (8 *or* 12 ounces) COOL WHIP Whipped Topping, thawed, divided

PLACE cake layers, top sides up, in 2 clean 8- or 9-inch round cake pans. Pierce cake with large fork at ¹/₂-inch intervals.

STIR boiling water into gelatin in medium bowl at least 2 minutes until completely dissolved. Carefully pour 1 cup of the gelatin over 1 cake layer. Pour remaining gelatin over second cake layer. Refrigerate 3 hours.

DIP 1 cake pan in warm water 10 seconds; unmold onto serving platter. Spread with about 1 cup of the whipped topping. Unmold second cake layer; carefully place on first cake layer. Frost top and side of cake with remaining whipped topping.

REFRIGERATE at least 1 hour or until ready to serve. Decorate as desired. Store leftover cake in refrigerator.   *Makes 12 servings*

Prep: 30 minutes   **Refrigerate:** 4 hours

Frozen Coffee Pie

¹/₂ cup hot fudge sauce
1 prepared chocolate flavor crumb crust (6 ounces or 9 inches)
1³/₄ cups cold milk
2 packages (4-serving size each) JELL-O Vanilla Flavor Instant Pudding & Pie Filling
2 tablespoons MAXWELL HOUSE Instant Coffee, any variety
1 tub (8 ounces) COOL WHIP Whipped Topping, thawed

HEAT hot fudge sauce as directed on jar. Pour into crust, tilting to cover bottom. Freeze 5 minutes.

POUR milk into large bowl. Add pudding mixes and instant coffee. Beat with wire whisk 1 minute or until well blended. Gently stir in whipped topping. Spoon into crust.

FREEZE 4 hours or until firm. Remove from freezer. Let stand 10 minutes before serving. Garnish with additional whipped topping, if desired. *Makes 8 servings*

Great Substitute: *For a delicious Frozen Mocha Mud Pie variation, substitute JELL-O Chocolate Flavor Instant Pudding & Pie Filling for the Vanilla Flavor.*

Prep: 15 minutes　**Freeze:** 4 hours

Baked Custard Fruit Tart

　2 teaspoons sugar
1½ cups milk
　2 eggs
　2 tablespoons flour
　1 package (4-serving size) JELL-O Vanilla Flavor Cook & Serve Pudding & Pie Filling (not instant)
　1 can (15 ounces) sliced peaches, drained

HEAT oven to 350°F. Grease 9-inch pie plate; sprinkle with sugar.

BEAT milk, eggs, flour and pudding mix until well mixed. Pour into prepared pie plate. Arrange peaches in pudding mixture.

BAKE 40 to 45 minutes or until filling is set and surface is golden brown. Cool on wire rack. Serve warm or cold, with whipped topping, if desired. *Makes 8 servings*

Prep: 10 minutes　**Bake:** 45 minutes

Berry Squares

1 package (12 ounces) pound cake, cut into 10 slices
3 tablespoons orange juice
2 pints fresh seasonal berries (strawberries, raspberries or blueberries)
2 tablespoons sugar
2½ cups cold milk
2 packages (4-serving size each) JELL-O Vanilla *or* Lemon Flavor Instant Pudding & Pie Filling
1 tub (8 ounces) COOL WHIP Whipped Topping, thawed, divided

ARRANGE cake slices in bottom of 13×9-inch pan. Drizzle cake with juice. Top with berries; sprinkle with sugar.

POUR milk into large bowl. Add pudding mixes. Beat with wire whisk 1 minute or until well blended. Gently stir in 1 cup of the whipped topping. Spoon mixture over berries in pan. Top with remaining whipped topping.

REFRIGERATE until ready to serve or overnight. Garnish as desired.

Makes 15 servings

Prep: 10 minutes

Make Ahead

This recipe is great for a crowd and is even better when prepared the night before!

Berry Square

Classic Twists

No Bake Pineapple-Ginger Cheesecake Squares

1 package (11.1 ounces) JELL-O No Bake Real Cheesecake
2 tablespoons sugar
1 tablespoon water
6 tablespoons butter or margarine, melted
1½ teaspoons ground ginger
1 can (20 ounces) crushed pineapple in juice, well drained, divided
1½ cups cold milk
1 teaspoon grated lemon peel

MIX Crust Mix, sugar, water, butter and ginger thoroughly with fork in 9×9-inch pan until crumbs are well moistened. Reserve 2 tablespoons. Press firmly onto bottom of pan using dry measuring cup. Spread ½ of the pineapple on the crust.

BEAT milk, Filling Mix and lemon peel with electric mixer on low speed until blended. Beat on medium speed 3 minutes. (Filling will be thick.) Spoon over pineapple in crust.

continued on page 52

No Bake Pineapple-Ginger Cheesecake Squares, *continued*

REFRIGERATE at least 1 hour. Top with remaining pineapple and reserved crumbs. Store leftover cheesecake, covered, in refrigerator.

Makes 8 servings

Great Substitute: *Orange peel can be substituted for lemon peel.*

Prep: 10 minutes   **Refrigerate:** 1 hour

Fluffy Cheesecake

1 package (8 ounces) PHILADELPHIA Cream Cheese, softened
⅓ cup sugar
1 tub (8 ounces) COOL WHIP Whipped Topping, thawed
1 prepared graham cracker crumb crust (6 ounces or 9 inches)

BEAT cream cheese and sugar in large bowl with wire whisk or electric mixer on high speed until smooth. Gently stir in whipped topping. Spoon into crust.

REFRIGERATE 3 hours or until set. Garnish as desired.

Makes 8 servings

Fluffy Caramel Pecan Cheesecake: *Beat cream cheese and sugar in large bowl with wire whisk until smooth. Gently stir in whipped topping. Spoon 1 cup cream cheese mixture into crust; spread evenly. Top with ⅓ cup KRAFT Caramel Topping and ¼ cup toasted pecans; spread evenly. Refrigerate 3 hours or until set. Garnish with additional caramel topping, whipped topping and pecans.*

Fluffy Cherry Cheesecake: *Prepare and refrigerate as directed above. Spoon 1½ cups cherry pie filling over top of pie.*

Fluffy Cranberry Cheesecake: *Beat in 1 cup whole berry cranberry sauce with cream cheese. Proceed as directed above.*

Prep: 15 minutes   **Refrigerate:** 3 hours

Fruit Whip

¾ cup boiling water
1 package (4-serving size) JELL-O Brand Orange Flavor Gelatin
½ cup cold orange juice
  Ice cubes
1 can (11 ounces) mandarin orange segments, drained (optional)

STIR boiling water into gelatin in large bowl at least 2 minutes until completely dissolved. Mix cold juice and ice cubes to make 1¼ cups. Add to gelatin, stirring until ice cubes are partially melted. Place in blender container; cover. Blend on medium speed 15 seconds. Pour into 6 dessert glasses or large glass serving bowl. Spoon in fruit.

REFRIGERATE 25 minutes or until set. The mixture sets with frothy layer on top and clear layer on bottom.   *Makes 6 servings*

Great Substitute: *Prepare as directed above, using any red flavor JELL-O Brand Gelatin and apple or cranberry juice.*

Prep: 10 minutes   **Refrigerate:** 30 minutes

Strawberry Shortcut

1 package (10 to 12 ounces) frozen pound cake, cut into 14 slices
3 cups strawberries, sliced, sweetened
1 tub (8 ounces) COOL WHIP Whipped Topping, thawed

PLACE 7 of the cake slices on individual dessert plates.

SPOON about 3 tablespoons of the strawberries over each cake slice. Top each with ¼ cup whipped topping. Repeat layers, ending with a dollop of whipped topping. Garnish as desired. Serve immediately.
          Makes 7 servings

Prep: 10 minutes

Lemon-Blueberry Pie Cups

6 vanilla wafer cookies
¾ cup canned blueberry pie filling
1 cup boiling water
1 package (4-serving size) JELL-O Brand Lemon Flavor Gelatin
¾ cup cold water
½ tub (8 ounces) COOL WHIP Whipped Topping, thawed

PLACE one vanilla wafer on bottom of each of 6 dessert cups. Top each wafer with 2 tablespoons pie filling. Set aside.

STIR boiling water into gelatin in large bowl at least 2 minutes until completely dissolved.

STIR in cold water. Refrigerate 10 to 15 minutes or until mixture is slightly thickened (consistency of unbeaten egg whites). Stir in ½ of the whipped topping until well blended. Spoon over pie filling in cups.

REFRIGERATE 2 hours or until firm. Garnish with remaining whipped topping, if desired.   *Makes 6 servings*

Great Substitutes: *Try using cherry or pineapple pie filling instead of the blueberry pie filling.*

Best of the Season: *Garnish each serving with fresh berries, if desired.*

Prep: 15 minutes   **Refrigerate:** 2¼ hours

Lemon-Blueberry Pie Cups

Chocolate Swirl Cheesecake

1 package (11.1 ounces) JELL-O No Bake Real Cheesecake
2 tablespoons sugar
1 tablespoon water
6 tablespoons butter or margarine, melted
2 squares BAKER'S Semi-Sweet Baking Chocolate
1⅔ cups cold milk, divided

STIR Crust Mix, sugar, water and melted butter thoroughly with fork in 9-inch pie plate until crumbs are well moistened. First press firmly against side of pie plate, using finger or measuring cup to shape edge. Press remaining crumbs firmly onto bottom using measuring cup.

MICROWAVE chocolate and 2 tablespoons of the milk in small microwavable bowl on HIGH 1½ minutes or until chocolate is almost melted. Stir until chocolate is completely melted; cool slightly.

BEAT remaining milk and Filling Mix with electric mixer on lowest speed until blended. Beat on medium speed 3 minutes. (Filling will be thick.) Stir ¼ cup of the filling into melted chocolate until well blended. Spoon remaining filling into crust. Place spoonfuls of chocolate mixture over filling in crust. Cut through cheesecake filling with knife several times to marbleize.

REFRIGERATE at least 1 hour. Garnish as desired.

Makes 8 servings

Prep: 15 minutes   **Refrigerate:** 1 hour

Tip

For a simple and delicious garnish for this cheesecake, melt 2 squares of BAKER'S Chocolate as noted above. Drizzle over top of cheesecake.

Chocolate Swirl Cheesecake

5-Minute JELL-O® Pudding Treats

JELL-O® Banana Split Cups

To 1 serving of JELL-O Vanilla Flavor Instant Pudding, add banana slices, a dollop of COOL WHIP Whipped Topping and your favorite sundae topping.

Warm JELL-O® Peanut Butter Cups

To 1 serving of JELL-O Chocolate Flavor Instant Pudding, add a spoonful of peanut butter. Press into pudding to cover. Microwave 30 seconds or until warm; stir gently. Top with COOL WHIP Whipped Topping.

Warm JELL-O® S'Mores

To 1 serving of JELL-O Chocolate Flavor Instant Pudding, add ½ crumbled graham cracker and 6 miniature marshmallows. Microwave 30 seconds or until warm; stir gently. Top with COOL WHIP Whipped Topping.

Warm JELL-O® Apple Pie Cups

To 1 serving of JELL-O Vanilla Flavor Instant Pudding, stir in 1 pinch of cinnamon, 2 tablespoons chunky applesauce and 1 crumbled vanilla cookie. Microwave 30 seconds or until warm; stir gently. Top with COOL WHIP Whipped Topping.

Two Tone Chocolate Cheesecake

1 package (11.1 ounces) JELL-O No Bake Real Cheesecake
2 tablespoons sugar
1 tablespoon water
6 tablespoons butter or margarine, melted
1 square BAKER'S Semi-Sweet Baking Chocolate
1 square BAKER'S Premium White Baking Chocolate
1½ cups cold milk

MIX Crust Mix, sugar, water and melted butter thoroughly with fork in 9-inch pie plate until crumbs are well moistened. First press firmly against side of pie plate, using finger or measuring cup to shape edge. Press remaining crumbs firmly onto bottom, using measuring cup.

MICROWAVE chocolates in 2 separate microwavable bowls on HIGH 1 minute or until chocolates are almost melted. Stir until chocolates are completely melted; cool slightly.

BEAT milk and Filling Mix with electric mixer on low speed until blended. Beat on medium speed 3 minutes. (Filling will be thick.) Slowly stir ½ of the filling mixture into each bowl of melted chocolate. Spoon semi-sweet chocolate cheesecake mixture into crust. Top evenly with white chocolate mixture.

REFRIGERATE at least 1 hour. Garnish as desired. Store leftover cheesecake in refrigerator.   *Makes 8 servings*

Tip: *For a marbled cheesecake, just after spreading the white chocolate cheesecake mixture on top of the semi-sweet chocolate cheesecake mixture, cut through batters with knife several times to marbleize.*

Prep: 15 minutes   **Refrigerate:** 1 hour

Two Tone Chocolate Cheesecake

Easy As Pie

Creamy Double Layer Pie

1¾ cups cold milk
2 packages (4-serving size each) JELL-O Instant Pudding & Pie
   Filling, any flavor
1 tub (8 ounces) COOL WHIP Whipped Topping, thawed, divided
1 prepared graham cracker or chocolate-flavor crumb crust
   (6 ounces or 9 inches)

POUR milk into large bowl. Add pudding mixes. Beat with wire whisk
1 minute or until well blended. Gently stir in ½ of the whipped
topping. Spoon into crust. Spread remaining whipped topping over
pudding in crust.

REFRIGERATE 3 hours or until set. Garnish as desired.

Makes 8 servings

Prep: 5 minutes   **Refrigerate:** 3 hours

Triple Berry Spring Pie

3 cups assorted berries
1 prepared graham cracker crumb or shortbread crumb crust
   (6 ounces or 9 inches)
1½ cups orange juice
½ cup sugar
2 tablespoons cornstarch
1 package (4-serving size) JELL-O Brand Gelatin, any red flavor
Thawed COOL WHIP Whipped Topping, optional

ARRANGE berries in bottom of crust.

MIX juice, sugar and cornstarch in medium saucepan over medium heat. Cook on medium heat, stirring constantly, until mixture comes to boil; boil 1 minute. Remove from heat. Stir in gelatin until completely dissolved. Cool to room temperature. Pour over berries in crust.

REFRIGERATE 3 hours or until firm. Garnish with Whipped Topping, if desired. Store leftover pie in refrigerator. *Makes 8 servings*

Prep: 20 minutes   **Refrigerate:** 3 hours

Great Stubstitute

*For an extra-delicious flavor boost,
use orange raspberry or orange
banana juice.*

Triple Berry Spring Pie

Candy Crunch Pie

2 cups cold milk
2 packages (4-serving size each) JELL-O Chocolate *or* **Vanilla Flavor Instant Pudding & Pie Filling**
1 tub (8 ounces) COOL WHIP Whipped Topping, thawed, divided
4 bars (1.5 ounces each) chocolate-covered wafer candy bars, cut into ¼-inch pieces, divided
1 prepared chocolate-flavor crumb crust (6 ounces or 9 inches)

POUR milk in medium bowl. Add pudding mixes. Beat with wire whisk 1 minute or until well blended. (Mixture will be thick.) Gently stir in ½ of the whipped topping. Reserve ¼ cup of the candy bars. Stir remaining candy into pudding mixture. Spoon into crust.

SPREAD remaining whipped topping over pudding in crust. Sprinkle top with remaining candy.

REFRIGERATE 4 hours or until set. *Makes 8 servings*

How To: *For best results, place candy bars in freezer or refrigerator prior to cutting.*

Great Substitute: *Substitute about 1 cup of your favorite candy bar (chopped) for the chocolate-covered wafer pieces.*

Note: *If making pie in advance, reserve chopped candy bar pieces to garnish just before serving. This will prevent them from becoming soggy in refrigerator.*

Prep: 5 minutes   **Refrigerate:** 4 hours

Strawberry Margarita Pie

1¼ cups crushed pretzels
¼ cup sugar
10 tablespoons butter or margarine, melted
1 can (14 ounces) sweetened condensed milk
1½ cups crushed or puréed strawberries
⅓ cup lime juice
1 tub (8 ounces) COOL WHIP Whipped Topping, thawed

MIX pretzels, sugar and melted butter in 9-inch pie plate. Press mixture onto bottom and up side of pie plate. Refrigerate.

MIX condensed milk, strawberries and lime juice in large bowl until well blended. Gently stir in whipped topping. Pour into crust.

FREEZE 6 hours or overnight until firm. Before serving, let stand at room temperature 15 minutes or until pie can be cut easily. Garnish with additional whipped topping and strawberries, if desired. Store leftover pie in freezer.   *Makes 8 servings*

Prep: 15 minutes   **Freeze:** 6 hours

How to

Dip pie plate into warm water, just to rim, for 30 seconds for easy serving.

Triple Layer Butterscotch Pie

2 squares BAKER'S Semi-Sweet Baking Chocolate, melted
¼ cup sweetened condensed milk
1 prepared chocolate flavor crumb crust (6 ounces or 9 inches)
¾ cup chopped pecans, toasted
1¾ cups cold milk
2 packages (4-serving size each) JELL-O Butterscotch Flavor Instant Pudding & Pie Filling
1 tub (8 ounces) COOL WHIP Whipped Topping, thawed, divided

POUR chocolate and sweetened condensed milk into bowl; stir until smooth. Pour into crust. Press nuts evenly onto chocolate in crust. Refrigerate 10 minutes.

POUR milk into large bowl. Add pudding mixes. Beat with wire whisk 1 minute or until well blended. (Mixture will be thick.) Spread 1½ cups of the pudding over chocolate in crust. Immediately stir ½ of the whipped topping into remaining pudding. Spread over pudding in crust. Top with remaining whipped topping.

REFRIGERATE 3 hours or until set. Garnish as desired.

Makes 8 servings

Great Substitute: *If you are a chocolate lover, simply substitute Chocolate Flavor Pudding for the Butterscotch Flavor.*

Prep: 15 minutes   **Refrigerate:** 3 hours

Triple Layer Butterscotch Pie

Easy Pudding Pie

2 cups cold milk
2 packages (4-serving size each) JELL-O Instant Pudding & Pie
    Filling, any flavor
1 tub (8 ounces) COOL WHIP Whipped Topping, thawed
1 prepared graham cracker or chocolate-flavor crumb crust
    (6 ounces or 9 inches)

POUR milk into large bowl. Add pudding mixes. Beat with wire whisk
1 minute or until well blended. Gently stir in whipped topping. Spoon
into crust.

FREEZE 3 hours or overnight. Let stand at room temperature
15 minutes before serving. Garnish with fruit or whipped topping.
Makes 8 servings

Creamy Lemon Pie: *Use Lemon Flavor Pudding and add ½ teaspoon
grated lemon peel.*

Prep: 5 minutes   **Freeze:** 3 hours

Apple Spice Cheesecake Pie

2 cups cold milk
2 packages (4-serving size each) JELL-O Cheesecake Flavor Instant
    Pudding & Pie Filling
½ teaspoon ground cinnamon
1 tub (8 ounces) COOL WHIP Whipped Topping, thawed, divided
1 prepared graham cracker crumb crust (6 ounces or 9 inches)
1 cup apple pie filling
2 tablespoons toasted chopped walnuts

POUR milk into large bowl. Add pudding mixes and cinnamon. Beat
with wire whisk 1 minute or until well blended. Gently stir in ½ of the
whipped topping. Spoon into crust.

SPOON pie filling evenly over pudding mixture.

REFRIGERATE 4 hours or until set. Just before serving, sprinkle with walnuts. Serve with remaining whipped topping.

Makes 8 servings

Prep: 15 minutes   **Refrigerate:** 4 hours

Layer After Layer Lemon Pie

      ⅓ **cup strawberry jam**
      1 **prepared graham cracker or shortbread crumb crust**
          (6 ounces or 9 inches)
      4 **ounces PHILADELPHIA Cream Cheese, softened**
      1 **tablespoon sugar**
      1 **tub (8 ounces) COOL WHIP Whipped Topping, thawed, divided**
  1½ **cups cold milk or half-and-half**
      2 **packages (4-serving size each) JELL-O Lemon Flavor Instant**
          Pudding & Pie Filling
      2 **teaspoons grated lemon peel**

SPREAD jam gently onto bottom of pie crust. Mix cream cheese and sugar in large bowl with wire whisk until smooth. Gently stir in ½ of the whipped topping. Spread on top of jam.

POUR milk into large bowl. Add pudding mixes and lemon peel. Beat with wire whisk 1 minute. (Mixture will be thick.) Gently stir in remaining whipped topping. Spread over cream cheese layer.

REFRIGERATE 4 hours or until set. Garnish with additional whipped topping, if desired.

Makes 8 servings

Best of the Season: *For an extra-special fruity flavor, place 1 cup strawberries into jam on bottom of crust; proceed as above.*

Take a Shortcut: *Soften cream cheese in microwave on HIGH 8 to 10 seconds.*

Prep: 20 minutes   **Refrigerate:** 4 hours

I could go for something

JELL-O ®
BRAND

Snack Time

JELL-O® Glazed Popcorn

  8 cups popped popcorn
  1 cup salted peanuts or cashews
¼ cup butter or margarine
  3 tablespoons light corn syrup
½ cup packed light brown sugar or granulated sugar
  1 package (4-serving size) JELL-O Brand Gelatin, any flavor

HEAT oven to 300°F. Line a 15×10×1-inch pan with foil or wax paper. Place popcorn and nuts in large bowl.

HEAT butter and syrup in small saucepan over low heat. Stir in sugar and gelatin; bring to a boil on medium heat. Reduce heat to low and gently simmer for 5 minutes. Immediately pour syrup over popcorn, tossing to coat well.

SPREAD popcorn in prepared pan, using two forks to spread evenly. Bake 10 minutes. Cool. Remove from pan and break into small pieces.

Makes about 9 cups

Prep: 10 minutes   **Cook:** 15 minutes

Fruity JELL-O® Cake

2 cups chopped strawberries
1 can (20 ounces) crushed pineapple, drained
1 package (8-serving size) *or* **2 packages (4-serving size each)**
  JELL-O Brand Strawberry Flavor Gelatin
3 cups miniature marshmallows
1 package (2-layer size) white cake mix
2 eggs

HEAT oven to 350°F.

ARRANGE fruit on bottom of 13×9-inch pan. Sprinkle with gelatin. Cover with marshmallows.

PREPARE cake mix as directed on package, omitting oil and using 2 eggs and water as specified. Spread batter over mixture in pan.

BAKE 50 to 55 minutes. Remove to rack; cool 15 minutes. Serve warm with thawed COOL WHIP Whipped Topping, if desired.

Makes 24 servings

Prep: 15 minutes   **Bake:** 55 minutes

How to

For ease in serving, line pan with foil; grease lightly. Proceed as directed. After baking and cooling 15 minutes, invert pan onto serving tray. Remove pan. Carefully remove foil from cake.

Fruity JELL-O® Cake

Citrus Parfaits

2 cups boiling water
1 package (4-serving size) JELL-O Brand Lime Flavor Gelatin
1 package (4-serving size) JELL-O Brand Lemon Flavor Gelatin
2 cups cold apple juice, divided
1 tub (8 ounces) COOL WHIP Whipped Topping, thawed

STIR 1 cup boiling water into each flavor of gelatin in separate bowls at least 2 minutes until completely dissolved. Stir 1 cup cold juice into each bowl. Pour into separate 9×9-inch pans.

REFRIGERATE 4 hours or until firm. Cut each pan into ½-inch cubes. Layer, alternating with flavors of gelatin cubes and whipped topping, into 8 dessert glasses. Garnish with additional whipped topping and berries, if desired. Store leftover dessert in refrigerator.

Makes 8 servings

Prep: 10 minutes   **Refrigerate:** 4 hours

Self-Layering Dessert

1 cup boiling water
1 package (4-serving size) JELL-O Brand Gelatin, any flavor
½ cup cold water
Ice cubes
½ cup thawed COOL WHIP Whipped Topping

STIR boiling water into gelatin in large bowl at least 2 minutes until completely dissolved. Mix cold water and ice cubes to make 1 cup. Add to gelatin, stirring until partially melted. Place in blender container; cover. Blend on medium speed 15 seconds. Add whipped topping; cover. Blend on high speed for 30 seconds.

POUR into 6 dessert glasses or a large glass serving bowl.

REFRIGERATE 45 minutes or until set. The mixture sets with a frothy layer on top and a clear layer on bottom.   *Makes 6 servings*

Great Substitute: *For an extra flavor burst, substitute cold juice for cold water.*

Prep: 10 minutes   **Refrigerate:** 45 minutes

Fruited Snack Cups

¾ **cup boiling water**
1 **package (4-serving size) JELL-O Brand Strawberry Flavor Gelatin,**
   or **any red flavor**
1 **cup cold orange juice**
   Ice cubes
¾ **cup thawed COOL WHIP Whipped Topping**
1 **can (11 ounces) mandarin orange segments, drained**

STIR boiling water into gelatin in large bowl at least 2 minutes until completely dissolved. Mix cold juice and ice cubes to make 1¼ cups. Add to gelatin, stirring until slightly thickened (consistency of unbeaten egg whites). Remove any remaining ice.

MEASURE 1 cup gelatin and stir in whipped topping with wire whisk until smooth. Pour about 2 tablespoons into each of 12 paper-lined or foil-lined muffin cups. Refrigerate about 25 minutes or until set but not firm (should stick to finger when touched and should mound). Stir fruit into remaining gelatin and carefully spoon over creamy layer, dividing evenly among muffin cups.

REFRIGERATE 3 hours or until firm.   *Makes 12 servings*

Take Along Tip: *This recipe can be made in a plastic container with a cover for a great take along school snack!*

Prep: 20 minutes   **Refrigerate:** 3 hours

Creamy Cantaloupe

  1 medium cantaloupe (about 3½ pounds)
¾ cup boiling water
  1 package (4-serving size) JELL-O Brand Gelatin, any flavor
½ cup cold orange juice
½ cup thawed COOL WHIP Whipped Topping

CUT melon in half lengthwise; remove seeds. Scoop out melon, leaving about 1-inch thick border of melon. Dice scooped out melon. Drain well. Cut thin slice from bottom of each melon shell to allow shells to stand upright, or place in small bowls.

STIR boiling water into gelatin in large bowl at least 2 minutes until completely dissolved. Stir in cold juice. Refrigerate 15 minutes or until slightly thickened (consistency of unbeaten egg whites). Gently stir in whipped topping. Stir in reserved diced melon. Pour into melon shells.

REFRIGERATE 3 hours or until firm. Cut into wedges.

Makes 8 servings

Prep: 15 minutes   **Refrigerate:** 3 hours

Food Facts

Choose a cantaloupe that is firm but yields to gentle thumb pressure at the blossom end. The melon should have a pleasant odor. Ripen cantaloupe at room temperature; refrigerate and be sure to use within 2 to 3 days.

Creamy Cantaloupe

Fruit 'n Juice Squares

1½ **cups boiling water**
  1 **package (8-serving size)** *or* **2 packages (4-serving size each)**
    JELL-O Brand Strawberry *or* **Cranberry Flavor Gelatin**
  1 **cup cold orange juice**
    Ice cubes
  1 **tub (8 ounces) COOL WHIP Whipped Topping, thawed, divided**
  1 **can (8¾ ounces) fruit cocktail, drained**

STIR boiling water into gelatin in large bowl at least 2 minutes until completely dissolved. Mix cold juice and ice cubes to make 1¼ cups. Add to gelatin, stirring until slightly thickened (consistency of unbeaten egg whites). Remove any remaining ice. Refrigerate 45 minutes.

RESERVE 1 cup gelatin; set aside. Stir ½ of the whipped topping into remaining gelatin until smooth. Pour mixture into 8-inch square pan. Refrigerate about 5 minutes until set but not firm (should stick to finger when touched and should mound). Stir fruit into reserved gelatin and carefully spoon over creamy layer in pan.

REFRIGERATE 3 hours or until firm. Cut into squares and garnish with remaining whipped topping.   *Makes 9 servings*

Storage Know How: *Keep gelatin refrigerated until ready to serve.*

Great Substitutes: *1 cup seasonal fresh berries may be substituted for canned fruit.*

Prep: 15 minutes   **Refrigerate:** 3¾ hours

Fruit 'n Juice Square

I could go for something

JELL-O ® BRAND

Kid Stuff

Cool Sandwich Snacks

10 whole graham crackers or chocolate-flavor graham crackers
½ cup chocolate fudge sauce
1 tub (8 ounces) COOL WHIP Whipped Topping, thawed
   Suggested Garnishes: Multi-colored sprinkles, assorted candies, finely crushed cookies, chocolate chunks, chopped nuts *or* toasted BAKER'S ANGEL FLAKE Coconut

SPREAD ½ of the graham crackers lightly with chocolate sauce. Spread whipped topping about ¾ inch thick on remaining ½ of the graham crackers. Press crackers together lightly, making sandwiches. Roll or lightly press edges in suggested garnish.

FREEZE 4 hours or overnight.   *Makes 10 sandwiches*

Make Ahead: *This recipe can be made up to 2 weeks ahead. Wrap well with plastic wrap and freeze.*

Prep: 15 minutes   **Freeze:** 4 hours

Cool Candy Cones

   6 flat-bottom ice cream cones
   1 tub (8 ounces) COOL WHIP Whipped Topping, thawed
   ⅓ cup multicolored sprinkles
   1 cup chopped candy bars (chocolate-covered wafer bars, peanut
      butter cups, etc.)

SPREAD top rims of ice cream cones with whipped topping. Roll in sprinkles.

STIR candy into remaining topping. Carefully spoon into prepared ice cream cones. Garnish tops with additional chopped candy, if desired. Serve immediately, or refrigerate or freeze until ready to serve.

Makes 6 servings

Berries and Cream: *Substitute 1 cup raspberries or chopped strawberries for the chopped candy bars.*

Prep: 10 minutes

Cool 'n Tropical Treat

   BREYERS Lowfat Yogurt, any flavor
   Low fat granola
   COOL WHIP LITE *or* FREE Whipped Topping, thawed
    Pineapple chunks, drained

ALTERNATE layers of yogurt, granola, whipped topping and pineapple chunks in glass or small bowl. Top with whipped topping.

Makes 1 serving

Best of the Season: *Use seasonal fresh berries in place of canned fruit, if desired.*

Prep: 5 minutes

Cool Candy Cones

JELL-O® Slime Drink

  1 cup boiling water
  1 package (4-serving size) JELL-O Brand Berry Blue Flavor Gelatin
  2 cups cold water
1½ cups cold lemonade
1½ cups cold lemon-lime carbonated beverage

STIR boiling water into gelatin in medium bowl at least 2 minutes until completely dissolved. Stir in cold water. Refrigerate 3 hours until soft set (gelatin breaks into small pieces when stirred with fork).

STIR gelatin with large fork or wire whisk until gelatin is broken into small pieces. Evenly divide lemonade and lemon-lime beverage among 6 glasses. Spoon gelatin into glasses and stir slightly.

Makes 6 servings

Make-Ahead: *The gelatin can be made ahead and used to make individual drinks.*

Prep: 10 minutes   **Refrigerate:** 3 hours

Cherry Cola Parfaits

2½ cups boiling carbonated cola beverage
  2 packages (8-serving size each) *or* 4 packages (4-serving size each) JELL-O Brand Cherry Flavor Gelatin
  1 tub (8 ounces) COOL WHIP Whipped Topping, thawed

STIR boiling beverage into gelatin in large bowl at least 2 minutes until completely dissolved. Pour into 13×9-inch pan. Refrigerate at least 3 hours or until firm. Dip bottom of pan in warm water about 15 seconds. Cut into ½-inch cubes.

LAYER gelatin cubes and whipped topping, in alternating layers, into 6 dessert glasses. Garnish with additional whipped topping, if desired.

Makes 6 servings

Take a Shortcut: *For an even quicker version, pour gelatin directly into 6 dessert glasses; refrigerate 3 hours or until set. Top with whipped topping.*

Prep: 10 minutes   **Refrigerate:** 3 hours

Fruit in a Cloud

1 tub (8 ounces) COOL WHIP Whipped Topping, thawed
**3 cups assorted fresh fruit, such as blueberries, grapes, sliced kiwi,
   melon, peaches and strawberries**

SPOON whipped topping evenly into 10 dessert dishes. Using back of spoon, make depression in center of each dish; spread whipped topping into bottom and up side of each dish.

REFRIGERATE until ready to serve.

SPOON fruit into center of whipped topping just before serving.

Makes 10 servings

Pudding in a Cloud: *Spoon 2 cups thawed COOL WHIP Whipped Topping into 6 dessert dishes as directed above. Pour 2 cups cold milk into medium bowl. Add 1 package (4-serving size) JELL-O Instant Pudding & Pie Filling, any flavor. Beat with wire whisk 2 minutes. Spoon pudding into center of whipped topping. Refrigerate until ready to serve.*

Prep: 10 minutes

Wiggly Giggly Worms

  ½ **cup boiling water**
   1 **package (4-serving size) JELL-O Gelatin Dessert, any flavor**
1½ **cups miniature marshmallows**
   8 **chocolate wafer cookies, finely crushed (optional)**
     Small candies

SPRAY 8-inch square pan with no stick cooking spray. Stir boiling water into gelatin in medium microwavable bowl at least 2 minutes until completely dissolved.

ADD marshmallows; microwave on HIGH 1 minute until marshmallows are puffed and almost melted. Stir mixture slowly until marshmallows are completely melted and mixture is smooth. (Creamy layer will float to the top.) Pour into prepared pan.

REFRIGERATE 1 hour. Dip bottom of pan in warm water for 15 seconds. Loosen edges with a knife. Cut into 16 ½-inch strips. Use candies for eyes on worms. Sprinkle cookie crumbs onto plate to resemble dirt. Place worms on top of dirt.   *Makes 16 worms*

Prep: 10 minutes   **Refrigerate:** 1 hour

Special Extra

Cookie cutters can be used to make different shapes.

Wiggly Giggly Worms

Peanut Butter-Banana Pops

1 package (16.1 ounces) JELL-O No Bake Peanut Butter Cup Dessert
1⅓ cups cold milk
1 medium banana, chopped

PLACE Topping Pouch in large bowl of boiling water; set aside.

POUR milk into deep, medium bowl. Add Filling Mix and Peanut Butter Packet. Beat with electric mixer on lowest speed 30 seconds. Beat on highest speed 3 minutes. (Do not underbeat.) Gently stir in Crust Mix and banana. Spoon into 12 paper-lined muffin cups.

REMOVE pouch from water. Knead pouch 60 seconds until fluid and no longer lumpy. Squeeze topping equally over mixture in cups, tilting pan slightly to coat tops. Insert pop sticks into cups.

FREEZE 2 hours or overnight until firm. Remove paper liners.

Makes 12 pops

Note: *Wooden pop sticks are sold at craft and hobby stores.*

Prep: 15 minutes   **Freeze:** 2 hours

Special Extra

For a more festive appearance, remove paper liners and gently roll side and top of each pop in seasonal colored sprinkles.

Peanut Butter-Banana Pops

Cosmic Clouds

1 tub (8 ounces) COOL WHIP Whipped Topping, thawed
1½ cups boiling water
1 package (8-serving size) *or* 2 packages (4-serving size each)
   JELL-O Brand Gelatin, any flavor
1 can (15.25 ounces) pineapple cosmic fun shapes, drained,
   reserving juice
Ice cubes

SPOON about ⅓ cup of the whipped topping into each of 10 dessert dishes. Using back of spoon, spread whipped topping into bottom and up side of each dish. Refrigerate until ready to fill.

STIR boiling water into gelatin in large bowl at least 2 minutes until completely dissolved. Mix reserved juice and enough ice cubes to make 2 cups. Add to gelatin, stirring until slightly thickened (consistency of unbeaten egg whites). If necessary, refrigerate to thicken gelatin. Stir in pineapple fun shapes. Fill center of whipped topping with gelatin mixture.

REFRIGERATE 3 hours or until firm.   *Makes 10 servings*

Prep: 15 minutes   **Refrigerate:** 3 hours

Family Fun

To create an even more exciting kids' dessert, stir a drop each of green and yellow food color into the COOL WHIP to tint the whipped topping sky-blue; then proceed as above.

I n d e x

Do The Cool Whip!
Cool Whip
Whipped Topping

I could go for something
JELL·O

9 3